SCHUYLER SPIRITUAL SERIES
Vol. 10

THE CHALLENGE
OF MIDLIFE

Anselm Grün, O.S.B.

Benedictine Mission House
P.O. Box 528
Schuyler, Nebraska 68661-0528

Originally published in German under the title
LEBENSMITTE ALS GEISTLICHE AUFGABE
(Münsterschwarzacher Kleinschriften: Bd. 13)
©1980 by Vier-Türme-Verlag
Münsterschwarzach, Germany
ISBN 3-87868-128-3

Translated by
Bill D. Bell and Quentin Kathol, OSB

USA English Edition
Copyright © 1993 by BMH Publications
All rights reserved.
ISBN 1-56788-004-5

THE CHALLENGE OF MIDLIFE

Anselm Grün, O.S.B.

Contents

Foreword

The Challenge of Midlife is a good example of how to make maximum use of both the old and new in our spiritual lives. In this case, the teachings of Johannes Tauler and Carl Gustav Jung are combined in such a way that they are mutually illuminating. Here we find a medieval mystic and a modern psychologist both commenting on an aspect of the human condition, and both of them contribute insights that penetrate far beneath the ordinary surface understanding of the problem, namely, the midlife crisis.

It seems to me, as a researcher who spends much time exploring the ancient monastic heritage, that the application of modern psychological insights is quite indispensable. For one thing, we citizens of the 20th century cannot dispense with psychology: it is our "native" way of looking at things. On the other hand, it is also very helpful to listen to someone from a very different time and mentality (i. e., Tauler, the medieval mystic) so as to expand our horizons and prevent them from becoming a psychological prison-house.

This particular topic, the phenomenon of midlife, appears to be one that demands particular attention at this time. With the population getting ever older, virtually everyone will experience this crisis, which Tauler shows us is not a crisis at all, but an opportunity.

When we listen to Jung, though, it is clear that unawareness of the dynamics of what is happening to us in this matter simply dooms us to a lot of unnecessary thrashing about and perhaps personal tragedy. He really seems to open a doorway to self-understanding.

Finally, one must commend the monks who made this book possible: Fidelis Ruppert, for his exposition of Tauler; Anselm Grün, for his study of Jung and his overall authorship of the booklet; and the Benedictine monks of Schuyler, Nebraska, for translating and printing the booklet in English. I'm sure it will help a lot of people as much as it helped me.

Terrence G. Kardong, O.S.B.

Introduction

The withdrawal of several brethren over the age of 40 affected our community very deeply. In exploring the reasons for leaving the community after almost twenty years of monastic life, we confronted the phenomenon of the "midlife crisis". A glance at the literature indicated to us that the midlife crisis seizes not only numerous priests and religious between the ages of 40 and 50, but others as well, forcing them to an existential crossroad which can lead them to abandon their calling. Indeed, for most individuals, the turning point of life presents a problem which, often enough, throws their previous life into a state of confusion. Career changes, withdrawal from familiar surroundings, divorces, nervous breakdowns, and a host of psychosomatic complaints are telltale signs of an unmanaged crisis in midlife.[1]

One theological study day, our community took the occasion of the departure of these brethren to consider the problems of midlife and their possible management. Two seminar papers provided a basis for communal discussion and the personal exchange of experiences in smaller groups. Abbot Fidelis Ruppert, O.S.B. read a paper on the ideas of the German mystic John Tauler (1300-1361), who describes the midlife crisis as a chance for spiritual growth. It was clear to us that we, as monks, must cope with the stresses of midlife primarily in a religious manner. Yet, in doing so, anthropological and psychological assumptions should not be discounted. Thus, as a supplement to the religious treatment of Tauler, I presented a report on the problems of midlife as seen from the psychological standpoint of C. G. Jung. The lively interest with which the ideas of Tauler and Jung were greeted by our own brethren and then by other religious men and women has led to our making them available to a wider audience. The section on Tauler goes back to the remarks made at the time by Abbot Fidelis and seeks to develop them somewhat further. The article on Jung appeared in *Erbe und Auftrag* 54 (1978).

The crisis of midlife is not simply a matter of adapting oneself anew to changed physical and psychic realities, of coping with the decline of bodily and intellectual energies, and of incorporating new wishes and desires which often emerge around the turning point of life. Rather, we are dealing here with a deeper existential crisis in which the meaning of the whole person is put to question: why do I work so much? why do I wear myself out without finding time enough for myself ? Why, how so, to what purpose, for what, for whom? These questions crop up more and more frequently in midlife and disrupt our former concept of living. The search for meaning is clearly a religious pursuit. Midlife is essentially a crisis of meaning and is therefore a religious crisis. Yet at the same time it holds out the possibility of finding a new meaning for our life.

The crisis of midlife shakes up the elements of human life in order to separate them out and arrange them anew. Seen from the perspective of faith, God is at work in this struggle. God brings about movement in the human heart in order to force it open and free it from all self-deception. This aspect of crisis as a work of grace is seldom seen in the voluminous literature on midlife. Yet this aspect is crucial. For the believer, the crisis of midlife is not something that strikes just from outside and for whose management faith can be employed merely as a source of strength. In the critical situation, God is acting. Therefore, the crisis is equally the locus of an intensive encounter with God and a new experience of him. It is a turning point on our path of faith, a point at which it's decided whether we make use of God in order to enrich our lives and develop ourselves, or whether we're ready to surrender ourselves to God in faith and give our lives over to him.

The studies on Tauler and Jung were begun, first of all, in view of our situation as monks. However, we learned that the questions we were dealing with must extend beyond solutions for monks, because, in the long run, everybody needs a religious approach to the crisis in midlife. Purely psychological methods and remedies do not go far enough. C.G.Jung, precisely as a psychologist, refers to non-psychological means: to the religious practices of fasting, of asceticism, of meditation, of liturgy. Jung expresses regret, however, that for many, the school of religion is no longer a help in managing their personal crises.

This small volume is intended to encourage a new discovery of the religious path as a path of healing, as a remedy for the wounds which life inflicts on us and which break open so painfully in the crisis of midlife. There is no going back, no denying all the lessons that psychology has given us. And yet we must go ahead on a path on which we allow ourselves, together with all the insights of psychology, to be led, ultimately, by Jesus Christ. Christ's way, which proceeds from the cross to the new life of the resurrection, is a path upon which we also, in a very human sense, become healthier and more mature; upon which, however, concepts like human self-realization and development of all one's talents are not of central importance. Instead, it's a matter of opening oneself and one's life to God, so that God can act in us and be strong in our weakness. Human self-realization and self-glorification are not the main concern but, rather, that in all things God may be glorified. Surely, an expression of the glorification of God *is* the healthy and mature individual, who, while dying, is clothed with the new life of resurrection, "so that the life of Jesus is made manifest in our mortal flesh" (II Corinthians 4:11).

I.
Surviving the Ordeal of Midlife
according to John Tauler

Tauler speaks often in his sermons about the fourth decade of life. The fortieth year represents a turning point. All the spiritual efforts we have made bear fruit only after the age of forty, and only then can we arrive at true peace of soul. In a sermon for the Ascension, Tauler takes the forty days between the Lord's resurrection and ascension and the additional ten days before the feast of Pentecost as a symbol of the spiritual development of a person.

> We may do as we please and embark on whatever we will, yet we shall never attain true peace or come close to being a saint until we reach our fortieth year. Up to then, we are preoccupied with many things, driven this way and that by natural impulses, and still often are ruled by them, although we may imagine that God is wholly in control of our life. Consequently, we cannot achieve true and perfect peace nor be in harmony with a heavenly model until the proper time. Then we must wait another ten years before the Holy Ghost, the Comforter, the Spirit who teaches all things, is fully bestowed on us.[2]

The seasons of one's life are not without meaning for the spiritual path one is on. For Tauler, the objective of the path is the ground of one's own soul. Scholars have much disputed the concept of *Seelengrund.* We have not gone into this learned discussion here, but simply take "ground of the soul" as an image of the innermost aspect of humanity, an expression for the ground in which all the forces of the soul are united, in which a person exists coherently, and in which God resides. One cannot reach the ground of the soul by one's own strength or by ascetic efforts – nor by frequent praying either. Not by *doing,* but only by *allowing,* do we come into contact with our innermost ground.

In the first half of life, though, we generally concentrate on our own doing. We would like to achieve something, not just in terms of worldly affairs, but also in terms of religion. Through spiritual exercises we would like to make progress on the road toward God. This is good in itself, for it shows that life is being appropriately ordered. Still, we do not attain the ground of the soul through our own striving, but only when we allow God to be at work within us. God deals with us through life itself and the experiences that life brings with it. God empties us by means of disappointments; God exposes our shallowness through our failures; God operates on us through the sufferings which God expects us to endure. The sense of being emptied out is but intensified during midlife.

At this juncture, everything depends on our letting God take over our own spiritual exertions, in order to be led by God through the emptiness and dryness of our own hearts, down into the ground of the soul, where we no longer meet our own images and feelings, but rather the true God. Hence, according to Tauler, the task of midlife is to allow ourselves to be emptied and stripped by God in order to be clothed anew with merciful grace. The crisis, then, is the decisive turning point at which one chooses whether to remain locked up within oneself or to allow God and God's grace to enter in. As described by Tauler in his sermons, we will trace the crisis and its management in six steps.

1. Crisis

Tauler observes that individuals who have led a religious life for years run into a spiritual crisis between their fortieth and fiftieth year. Everything they previously practiced in terms of religious exercises, contemplation, personal and communal prayer, choral office, devotions – all seem suddenly meaningless. No longer do they take pleasure in these things; they feel empty, exhausted, dissatisfied.

> All the pious thoughts and lovely images, all the joy and jubilation, all that God has given us now seems coarse and absurd. We will banish this altogether, especially since we have no more appetite for it and wish no longer to be part of it. We do not like it anymore, but what we do long for, we do not possess, so we find ourselves in a dilemma and are caught up in great woe and adversity.[3] (174)

13

The two horns of this dilemma are that we can no longer accomplish much through our usual religious practices, yet also we do not know what is best for us. We lose the familiar, but the new is not yet present. And the danger exists that, along with traditional religious practices, we will throw faith itself overboard, since we find no way to get closer to God. All the spiritual efforts on which we previously relied are now frustrated. The security of external forms is gone. Thus, in disappointment, we waver on the brink of turning away from God.

For Tauler, however, this crisis is actually the work of God's grace. God leads us into crisis, into such a bind. And God has a purpose for doing so. God desires to bring us to the truth, to usher us to the ground of the soul. Here Tauler uses the image of God turning a house inside out and upside down in order to find a coin (the drachma), that is, the ground of the soul.

> Suppose a person comes into this house and there seeks God, but finds the house in disarray. Then God starts seeking that person and ransacks the house like somebody conducting a search: God throws one thing here and another there until God finds the object being looked for. (172)

Overturning the previous arrangement of the house allows us to discover our own ground and contributes far more to our spiritual maturity than all our own endeavors.

14

So if it were possible, and if nature could stand being overturned seventy-seven times by day and night – if we would endure that and could deliberately stay in the midst of it, we would gain far more than anything we ever understood or was ever given. If we could allow this topsy-turvy experience to happen to us, we would be led much further along by far than in all the works and precepts and statutes that anybody ever invented or yet imagined. (173)

Frequently, though, we react wrongly to the crisis into which God has led us. We fail to recognize that God is doing something to us and that it is important to allow God's activity to take its course. Tauler describes several different ways of reacting wrongly to the crisis.

2. Flight

I can flee from the crisis of midlife in three ways. The first is a refusal to look within myself, not confronting the turmoil within but exteriorizing it. Filled outwardly with impatience, I want to improve everything: other people, existing structures, established institutions. When God makes me restless, when God turns my house upside down, when God approaches me and with the light of grace

begins to touch me, I ought to wait where I am. Instead, I renounce the *Seelengrund*, turn the house on its head, and want to run off to a place like Trier or God knows where, and reject the testimony (of the Spirit within me) because of my penchant for outwardly visible activity. (177)

Not wishing to reform myself, I propose now to reform the house. I project dissatisfaction with myself on to objects outside and block the entrance to the ground of my soul with exterior reforms. I am so strongly reform-minded and busy with external improvements that I barely notice how my inner being fails to keep step with the exterior change. Shifting the struggle outward relieves me of the duty of struggling with myself.

A second kind of flight is exemplified by clinging to external religious practices. Instead of relating to others, to my surroundings, I remain by myself. But I hold fast to my beloved external forms. I flee from that *inner* confrontation into the world of things to do. Instead of listening inwardly and paying attention to the hidden "paths from within", I am determined to remain on the "ordinary, broad thoroughfares."

As Tauler explains, many people do it the wrong way around: they give up and

become wholly absorbed in external practice and proficiency, behaving just like the person who ought to be going to Rome, i.e., inland, and then heads west down toward Holland; the further they go, the more they stray from the path. And when such people later return, they are old and their heads hurt, and they can no longer pay their dues despite their enterprise and fury. (177)

A third kind of flight is the stratagem of translating one's inner unrest into ever-changing life-styles. The turbulence within propels such people now to this and now to that religious practice:

> When they are disturbed from within, they are immediately up and away: into another country or another city. But if they're not able to do this, they at least adopt – again, of course, only superficially – another pattern of life: now to become a poor man, then to live in a hermitage, then to enter a monastery. (178)

Again, they expect a resolution of the inner crisis through external forms. However, in this case, they throw the traditional forms overboard and look for new ones.

This observation by Tauler is confirmed today in the conduct of many people who are always trying out new forms of meditation. They get carried away first by this one, then by that. When the first enthusiasm slackens, they change over to a different one, which now becomes the *ne plus ultra*. And since they don't persevere with any one form, they never find their own ground. They don't face up to their own unrest, they don't bear up with it, they don't listen to God's voice summoning them right through this ordeal into their own inner selves. Thus, instead of changing themselves inwardly, they pursue new external arrangements.

> This trouble has caused many to run to Aachen, to Rome, among the poor, and to hermitages. But the more they run, the less they find. And quite a few lapse again into rational metaphors and play around with them – all because they refuse to suffer through this anguish. As a result, they plunge into utter despair. (178)

The reaction of flight is understandable, for few are told about the positive role of crisis in midlife. Feeling very insecure, most people just react to their predicament, often mindlessly. Therefore, it is important to be aware of the step-wise character of the spiritual life. Each step has its function. The period of midlife is a crucial step on the pathway to God and self-realization – a painful step which many therefore do not freely admit and to whose approach they react with the defense-mechanism of flight. The restless activity characteristic of many people at this age is often an unconscious flight from the inner crisis. However, since most of them are left alone in their crisis, they find no alternative. It follows, then, that we need spiritually-experienced counselors who can help these people in their crisis and accompany them along this very difficult mile on the road to both human and spiritual maturity.

3. Holding Back

Another form of reacting to the crisis of midlife is fixation, i.e., a retreat from the challenge of taking the next developmental step, a holding fast to our former way of life. On the psychological level, it manifests itself as an obstinate sticking to principles; we take shelter behind principles in order to conceal our inner fear. In the religious domain, the reaction of holding back shows up in our exaggerated concern about past devotional exercises. We faithfully fulfill our religious duties, go to worship services regularly on Sundays, and recite our daily prayers. We attend pedantically to the exact performance of religious duties. Yet, in spite of it all, we make no interior headway. We become ever more hard-hearted and unkind; we complain about others, condemn their moral or religious laxity, and fancy ourselves as devout Christians who must show others how they should lead the Christian life. In spite of all the zeal evidenced by such people, one nevertheless has the impression that they radiate nothing of the love and goodness of Christ. They generate little enthusiasm. Everything smells of pedantry and narrowness. They are petty, joyless, harsh in judgment, self-righteous.

By strictly adhering to religious principles and practices, the person holding back seeks to cover up the inner crisis and to disguise the fear which the crisis evokes. This at root is the fear that God could wrest from my hand all the portraits I've made of myself and of God, and push me in such a way that my self-erected edifice of life would collapse.

Tauler again and again inveighs against anxious attachment to external principles and rules. He intends by his sermons to expose the constrictions of the heart that one often meets with, especially in devout individuals. The forms so tenaciously and fearfully clung to, Tauler calls *idols*. By this he means that many people 'sit' on their *idols* as Rachel once protected her household gods (Genesis 31:34). They cherish their idols in order to avert their encounter with the real and true God.

> Many people are so pleased with their ways (i.e., their kind of living and their kind of piety) that they surrender to no one, not to God or anyone, and protect themselves like the apple of their eye in not yielding themselves over to God. If our Lord comes with an admonition, directly or indirectly, they at once put their guard up and pay it not the least attention. (152)

These people fight against everything by which God could make a direct appeal to them and call them into question. They hold fast to their practices and set them up as barriers between themselves and God. Their security, their religious conviction, is more important than a personal encounter with God, whom they keep at a distance for fear God might be dangerous. God might show them, for example, what their situation really is and the underlying motives of their conformity. Perhaps, even, God could reveal their religious activities as self-insurance, holding up to view their devious intentions and desires, as well as the vain attempt to suppress their fear.

Thus, instead of *being* religious, they take cover behind religious deeds. These things they do so as to avoid hearing from God that they aren't really devout after all, but by their actions are seeking only themselves, their security, their self-justification, their spiritual wealth. They stick obstinately to pious practices without noting that these alone do not make them devout. They become embittered in their self-styled goodness but remains beyond the reach of God's direct appeal that would call them to the truth.

This position is so typical of the Pharisees! Unfortunately, it is the position taken also by many so-called good Christians who don't dare to believe in the real God and the process of being continually transformed by God. Tauler says of these pseudo-pious that they would be content with closed cisterns rather than drink from the living fountain of God. And he laments how many spiritual people there are

> who have quit the living waters completely and who, deep down, have so little true light and life but only a great deal of rote religion instead. Despite their exterior deeds and methods and rules, they lag very far behind.

Everything is brought from the outside in, through sensible sounds and images, while from the interior ground, where spirituality should leap out and gush forth, there proceeds absolutely nothing. They are truly like cisterns, containing nothing that springs from the earth but only what is collected from the outside and then flows away as quickly as it came. And what may pass for religion in these people is nothing but a batch of rules and methods which they have established according to their own judgment. They neither turn to their ground, where no fountain or thirst exists, nor do they strive to go forward. As long as they have completed their agenda in their own way, i.e., from the outside to the inside by means of the senses, they are extremely satisfied. The cisterns they have made suit them very well, but for God they have no thirst. The font of living water they leave untouched. (154)

Tauler concludes this unflattering description by saying:

All the perfunctoriness that collects in these cisterns becomes foul and putrid and finally dries up, so that nothing remains in the ground but pride, self-will, hardheartedness, rash judgment, harsh words, and bad manners . . . (154f)[4]

With external busyness, pious diligence and religious activism, we would like to conceal the fact that we have no relationship to our own ground – even that God is a stranger to us. We mean to take possession of God when we perform certain spiritual exercises. We wish to conscript God into our own religious program. The basis of this posture is the fear of the living God. Because we are afraid God could destroy our edifice of protection and self-justification – thus exposing ourselves as naked and destitute before the real God – we attempt, through irreproachable behavior, to erect a bulwark which God cannot penetrate. Performance of duty, then, springs not from a sincere and loving heart which God has moved and touched, but from an anxious devotion to self. We choose justification by works, for fear of submitting to the divine judgment and of falling too trustingly into God's loving arms. Clasping self to self, we shrink from the faith which entails the giving of self to God.

Tauler does not advise giving up spiritual exercises. On the contrary, external forms of piety are good, insofar as they have the inner person as their objective and help to release that person from worldly attachments.[5] Tauler exhorts young people above all to active forms of love, to do visible things which lead to the love of God.[6] Yet the danger still exists that we overestimate the effect of our own actions and that our exercises "engage us so completely that we are never able to enter into ourselves."[7] For Tauler, the 40's are a turning point in the assessment of one's external practices. He cites for support Pope Gregory the Great, who in his biography of St. Benedict states that "the priests of the Old Covenant became custodians of the temple no earlier than the age of fifty; as long as they were below this age, they were only representatives of the temple and were preoccupied with chores."[8] Below age forty or fifty, devotional exercises are a necessary mainstay so that we can grow spiritually and draw closer to God. Yet during this time, says Tauler, "we should not, either inwardly or outwardly, place too much confidence in peace, in self-denial, or even in self-mastery, because all this is still overly intermingled with nature."[9] When we, after the age of fifty, cling excessively to external practices and consider them more important than contact with the ground of our souls eventually become a dried-up cistern. We become engrossed in external activities without ever feeling, deep down, the inner urging of God.

4. Self-knowledge

The crisis of midlife introduces the challenge of self-knowledge, which is, at the same time, an aid in dealing with the crisis. When God's grace has impinged on us and turned the constructs of our former thought and life upside down, we are given the chance to know ourselves, not only outwardly, but in the very ground of our soul, where our essential nature lies hidden. For Tauler, the pathway to self-knowledge turns inward, descending to the ground of our being. Since, however, honest awareness of the hidden self is painful to begin with – because we discover unsparingly what darkness and evil, what cowardice and falsehood also lurk there – we gladly avoid it. Tauler describes in drastic metaphor the condition of those who shirk the responsibility of self-knowledge.

> Children, how do you account for the fact that there's no way for you to gain access to your ground? This is the reason: because many a thick, ugly hide has been pulled over it, thick as an ox's brow, and so covering up your inner being that neither God nor you yourself can enter. Mind you, many people are wearing thirty or forty hides: thick, coarse, black hides like bearskins. (189)

Again and again we observe how hard it is to get close to many people. We can point out their shortcomings, but they pretend not to hear. We can charitably call their attention to modes of conduct which are repellent, but in vain. They have no inkling of their real condition. And, with his image of ox hide, Tauler suggests that such people have so little connection with their own reality that it's impossible even for God to get through. Their inner being is covered over, made inaccessible both to themselves and to God. Similarly, they learn nothing from the experiences which God sends them – whether positive or negative. They've become rigid. They regard all events as subject to their own validation. They have a sharp eye for the weaknesses of others, but as for their own weaknesses, they are blind. Psychologists have a name for this blindness: projection. Having projected my weaknesses onto others, I can no longer recognize them in myself. I am blind to my own condition. Projection manifests itself in complaining about others, in condemning and criticizing. Tauler takes it as a "characteristic of the false friends of God that they judge other people but not themselves. God's true friends are the opposite: they judge no one but themselves." (191)

Self-knowledge is mostly unpleasant for us. It rips the mask from our faces and reveals the person within. It therefore stands to reason that many would like to avoid the pain of self-scrutiny. In the crisis of midlife, however, God intervenes and leads us gradually to a better self-under-standing. Tauler considers it a sign that the Holy Spirit is at work when this self-understanding begins to occur. We find ourselves more and more distressed, convulsed to the inner core, by the same Holy Spirit who lays bare whatever is false and deceitful within us:

> With this passover of the Spirit, a great upheaval rumbles throughout the human soul. The clearer and truer and more undisguised the passover is, the faster, stronger, truer and more audible is also the movement, the motivation and the conversion going on inside

us, and the more clearly we recognize how much we have been holding back. (192)

As soon as we get to the ground, we experience a rude awakening:

> Oh, what deceit we shall find there when we tread upon the ground! What at present appears as great holiness, shall be re-discovered as falsehood! (191)

We talk of having to protect individuals from the upheavals of midlife. Tauler, on the other hand, sees them as the work of the Holy Spirit. We should allow ourselves to be unsettled by the divine Spirit so that we can break through to our ground and make contact with our own authenticity. We should trust enough to allow the tower of our self-complacency and self-righteousness to tumble down upon us; we should yield ourselves completely to the work that God is doing in the midst of this tough situation:

> Beloved friends, sink, sink into the ground, into your nothingness, and permit the tower (the cathedral of self-complacency and self-righteousness) with all its levels to collapse on you! Let the demons of hell march over you! Heaven and earth and all creation – everything shall serve you wondrously! You have only to descend and the best of everything shall be given to you. (193)

It's a brave word of advice that Tauler speaks here. We should permit even the hellish demons to trample over us, in the confidence that God will be our escort through the time of tribulation.

Self-knowledge is set in motion by the Holy Spirit. But we, too, must deliver our own part to the bargain. Tauler offers various helps along the way to mature self-realization. He describes how we should carefully observe and test our actions and our letting go, our fondest thoughts and desires, and the particular weaknesses of our nature. Self-examination needs to be practiced:

> Children, it requires an immense, singular effort to correctly discern your basic character; to that end, you must study day and night and use your imagination; you must control yourself and discover the drives and motivations underlying your various activities. And with all your strength, you should set your actions aright and align yourself directly to God; then you will be telling no lies, for every good work that you do for something other than God is a lie. Everything is idol-worship whose aim is not God. (195)

The method that Tauler recommends here is imaginative "picturing", which modern-day psychology employs as a technique for self-realization. The individual allows images to emerge from one's fantasy, from the ground, from the subconscious, and then observes them. As a result it's often possible to uncover the actual bedrock and roots of our thoughts and actions. With the help of this technique, as Tauler advises, we should inquire again and again as to the ultimate motives of our actions, whether we are putting ourselves, or God, at the center. We should examine ourselves as to whether we are attached to external things, to our successes, to the role we play, to our office or vocation, to our property, to the formal aspects of our piety, to our reputation as good Christians. We should identify our idols – and as soon as we've done so, we should try to break away from them. We must let go of all the things to which we cling in order to be in touch solely with God's will.

The perception that, during midlife, God leads us to a painful self-appraisal has been noted, too, by Carlo Carretto. He writes of this experience:

> It normally happens when we are about forty years old. Forty years: a major liturgical date in life, a biblical date, date of the noonday demon, date of one's second youth, a time of decision . . . . This is the date, chosen by God, when we are put with our backs against the wall – we who up to this point have tried to wriggle through under the cloudy mist of a "half-yes and half-no". Along with setbacks come disillusionment, disgust, darkness, and, deeper still, the witnessing or experiencing of sins. We discover who and what we are: a poor thing, a frail, fragile creature, a mixture of pride and of malice, a creature of inconsistency, of laziness, of illogicality. This human wretchedness knows no limits, and God lets us taste it to the dregs . . . .

But that isn't enough! At bottom lies that guilt which is both decisive and extensive, even when it's concealed . . . . We incur it only with great effort and perhaps only after a long time, though it takes but a moment. At any rate, it is sufficiently alive in our consciousness to burden us and weigh heavier upon us than all the things we normally confess. I'm speaking of the attitudes which envelop our whole life like a sphere and which are always present in what we do and what we leave alone; sins which we cannot simply shake off; things which are hidden from us for the most part and still have us completely in their grip: laziness and cowardice, deceit and vainglory, vices from which our prayers can never be entirely free. Things such as these weigh heavily upon our whole existence. [10]

This quotation indicates that Tauler's insight does not stand alone, nor is it restricted to mystics. It affects everyone who attempts to lead a spiritual life. Thus it is important to be well versed in the laws of the spiritual life, in order to be able to help those who, right now, are going through this crisis as a step in their religious development.

5. Detachment

In addition to self-knowledge, Tauler proposes yet another support for dealing with the crisis of midlife. We may call it detachment. He doesn't have in mind here a stoic kind of resignation or composure which forbids anything to make one upset, but rather the capacity to let go and surrender. For Tauler, detachment is what the Holy Scriptures call self-denial, the giving up of one's own will in order to merge it with God's will. It has a dynamic aspect and implies a forward movement toward God.

The human being must give up a great deal in order to improve one's circumstances. The person must forsake evil, self-will, high-handedness; but sometimes also the good, insofar as it hinders progress. For the good can be the enemy of the better and can prevent one from forging ahead on the path to God. Tauler illustrates this with the image of the bride who is divested of her old clothes and is bathed, "in order to be more gloriously clothed with new garments by the heavenly bridegroom." (198) Among the old clothes Tauler understands not only those soiled by sin, but also those "good clothes which are taken off the bride simply because they are old." (198) He means by this the good practices and common virtues which need to be replaced by a better practice, by a higher virtue.

There are forms of religious expression appropriate for every age. Without examining it again, we should not hold on to a practice which was a good choice for youth. And if a previous practice now seems empty and unfruitful to us experiencing the midlife crisis, it is not because we were wrong to pursue it before, but because God wants to tell us by this disappointment that we must now look for other forms which better correspond to the current developmental phase of our spiritual life.

Perhaps a higher level of praying is called for. Thus, instead of praying in long monologues which tire me out, I may have to learn to be silent before God. Instead of devouring more and more devotional books, perhaps I ought to simplify my prayer; or, similarly, I ought to dispense with constantly wanting to experience new spiritual highs and religious feelings and, in place of that, become quite ordinary before God, living in God's presence without being able to say much about it. Many individuals get into a midlife religious crisis by thinking that they can apply the desire for conquest, at which they were successful in professional life, to the religious life as well. They want to catch hold of religious experiences whenever possible and, metaphorically speaking, amass a personal spiritual fortune. Dullness and disappointment in prayer are an indication that I must give up my search for the esoteric, must renounce the quest for ownership and just be very simple before God. What matters most is that I surrender myself to God totally, without always demanding some gift in return, such as contentment, rest, security, or religious gratification.

To detachment belongs also the willingness to suffer, to endure. Detachment does not mean that I have found the quiet life and now enjoy it; just the opposite, I am willing to release it from my hand. I am ready to let God lead me into the tumult. "True peace is born only from the discord of the purifying storm." (216) Enduring the trial and the suffering that goes with it is therefore incumbent upon me:

> Stay by yourself and don't run away; hold out through your sufferings and don't be looking out for something else! Too many people, standing in the midst of inner desolation, always react by seeking some means of escape. Or they go about complaining or questioning the teachers and are even more misled. Have no doubt about it: after the darkness comes the sunshine, the dawn of a bright day. (217)

Tauler says repeatedly that I am not supposed to break away from the hardship; I must simply wait. I can not get loose by my own power. There's nothing I can do but wait, confident that God will guide me to a new spiritual maturity. Yes, I must trust that God never lets me fall into deep distress without pursuing with me a positive objective. Relying on God to lead, I must now be ready to hand over the reins and allow God to be fully in charge. In the crisis of midlife a transfer of command needs to take place: no longer I, but God shall lead. God is already at work in the crisis and I should put nothing in the way of God's finishing up in me what God has begun.

Tauler never tires of helping his listeners understand that the Holy Spirit has provoked the crisis and that by putting me through the ordeal of adversity, the Holy Spirit can meanwhile act upon me. My duty now is not to hinder the Holy Spirit's work, but to

> remain open and ready, giving the Holy Spirit adequate work space in which to begin. Very few do this – not even those wearing religious garb whom God has hitherto chosen. (180)

Tauler can employ extremely vivid images to describe the means which the Holy Spirit may use to change me inwardly and create me anew. Thus, alluding to with Matthew 10:16, he cites the ingenuity of the snake:

> When it senses that it is beginning to age, to shrivel and to stink, it seeks a place where two stones are lying close beside one another, and there it drags itself tightly through so that its old skin is stripped off, while under it a new skin has already developed. Humans ought to do exactly the same with their old skin, including everything they have from nature. No matter how great or good it may be, it is surely out of date and contains definite imperfections; for this reason it should be dragged through the gap between two stones which lie very close to one another. (215)

In order to enter the ground of our souls and grow to maturity, we in our 40's must wriggle through the narrowness of the two stones; we cannot continually chase after the newest formulas for human and spiritual development. This would only be a flight from adversity. Sometime or other we must muster the courage to go through the narrow gap, even though we lose our old skin or suffer wounds and abrasions in the process. Decisions restrict choices. Yet without this tight ordeal to go through, we cannot be renewed and attain spiritual adulthood. The external person must be worn away so that day by day the inner person is created anew (II Corinthians 4:16).

If we take the words of Tauler seriously and see that God is at work, then the crisis of midlife loses its ominous aspect of danger. We need not shrink away in fear. Indeed, we can accept it positively, as a chance to take a step forward and get closer to God. What is required, then, as long as the crisis lasts, is the willingness to let God carry out the work. Often enough, God's action causes us pain. Then it's a question of putting up with God, of enduring what God sends us without falling apart inside. This attitude demands a lot of anyone who was accustomed to taking personal charge of everything. We run the built-in risk of wanting to regain control of the crisis, of trying to play the active part in it, and also of being determined to accelerate the process. Perhaps we recognize our chance and desires to make use of it by stepping in ourselves and throwing traditional forms overboard. Tauler warns of arbitrary intervention in what

God is doing. We are not allowed to interfere with God's work in and through the ordeal, nor to give up previous religious practices on our own initiative, but only when God so ordains and urges us:

> As to the ways and means which mainly dispose a person, outwardly and inwardly, for good works and the love of God, these the person ought not to give up until they diminish by themselves. (182)

One must learn, slowly at first, to make room for the activity of God. It's all too easy to take over again the planning of one's life and practice of religion. We distrust all passivity and are afraid to hand over the reins. Because it was good up until now to define and shape the life we live, there's a natural tendency to continue on in this fashion. Even so, while it's appropriate for youth to practice skills and to set up agendas and goals, the mature older person must defer to God, adapting step-by-step to whatever God wills and transferring to God the role of supervision. This demands the oblation of one's own heart.

6. The Birth of God

The problems and anxieties which characterize the crisis of midlife are, for Tauler, simply the labor pains which herald the birth of God in the person. God compels the person in the tumult of this crisis to turn to the ground of one's own existence, to recognize therein one's own helplessness and weakness, and to surrender entirely to God's Holy Spirit. When the person lets loose of everything that may hinder God's unseen creative action, then God can be born in the ground which has been so strenuously prepared. And, according to Tauler, the birth of God in humanity is the goal of the spiritual path:

> Trust me! No anguish stirs within you but that God intends to produce a new birth. And be aware: whatever quiets or relieves the anguish or the stress, it is something coming to birth in you. And then the birth takes place, be what it may, God or creature. But mind you now, if a creature relieves you of the anguish, call it whatever you will, it thwarts the birth of God in you completely. (217)

With Tauler's warning, the danger of the crisis again becomes clear. One is tempted to relieve the pressure oneself, e.g., by turning outward, by busy activity, by latching onto religious forms, by external changes. But these are all created, self-made things which would hinder God from being born in us. Therefore we must allow God to assume the burden alone, which means: giving God the chance to act, giving our future over to God. God alone can free us from the burden.

> Come what may, from outside or inside: let everything fester out. Seek no consolation, for God is surely redeeming you. Keep yourself free for this to happen and leave everything up to God. (217)

The prerequisite for God to be born in us is the turn inwards. The soul

> should establish peace and innermost quiet, close itself up, conceal and protect the mind from invasion by the sensory world, and prepare a silent place within, a sanctuary of inner repose.[11]

In such a state of silence God's word can be heard and absorbed. Therein, too, is the human birth of God fulfilled, as was the case of Mary, of whom Augustine said: "More blessed was she that God was born spiritually in her soul, than that God was born physically from her body."[12]

With the concept of the birth of God, so typical of German mysticism, Tauler suggests that the person is opened up for God: able to encounter God, to be inwardly changed by God, and to live wholly from God's Spirit. No longer is God just an authority figure who looks for obedience to the law, no longer the conceptual ideal to be strived after. God is now perceived as intrinsic to the person, who, having experienced God's presence so near, continues to live from this experience. Life from God is centered no longer on the will as the means by which one proposes to fulfill God's commandments. It springs up, rather, from a heart captivated by God, a heart which, owing to God's nearness, has become peaceful and serene, mature and wise, generous and full of love.

So the crisis of midlife does have a purpose! It's an excellent opportunity for us to break through to a genuine human existence and to take a decisive step forward on the pathway to God.

If we understand that the turmoil besetting us and the birth of God are interconnected, as Tauler has shown, we will then be able to react differently when the first signs of the crisis appear. We won't, in a panic, think that every possible psychological method must be tried in order to pull through. We will see, rather, the great spiritual challenge of staying with the crisis and of listening attentively to what God wants to say to us in the midst of it. We must not shield ourselves from it with the many defense mechanisms we have at hand. We also need not run away. Instead, with confidence and trust, we can allow God to act upon us. We can put up with the fact that God turns our house upside down and, like a whirlwind, throws into disarray the interior order we thought we had. Better than bewailing our predicament, we would be grateful for it: that God is acting upon us, that God breaks up our rigidity for the coming of the Spirit, who would like more and more to transform our hearts.

II.
Problems of Midlife
according to C. G. Jung

Carl Gustav Jung approaches the tensions of midlife from a different point of view than that of the mystic-preacher John Tauler. Jung is a psychologist and, as such, limits himself to the methods of empirical science. The more philosophical and theological conclusions he leaves to the theologians.

Nevertheless, as a psychologist, he sees religion as a real phenomenon, too; again and again he encounters it among his patients. One can hardly examine a person's psyche without observing also its attempts to answer the question of meaning by use of religious systems and images. Jung takes a scientific interest in religious interpretations only to the extent that they contribute to the health of the human soul. Whether or not a transcendental reality lies behind the religious images, as a scientist, he cannot say. As a non-professional, though, he has often enough acknowledged this reality.

It may surprise us that Jung, coming from psychology, arrives at conclusions similar to Tauler's. This suggests that the correctly perceived religious path is also the correct one psychologically. Psychology supplies us with criteria to distinguish, within religious practice, between defective forms and those that are healthy. On the other hand, it may never assume the role of measuring religion by non-religious standards. Still, every religion must at least pose the psychological question: to what extent does religion, with all its dogmas and spiritual discipline, make a person emotionally healthy or sick? Religion has always understood and described itself as a path leading to salvation – not only in a strictly other-worldly sense, but in a plainly human sense as well.

In the wake of Sigmund Freud, psychology concentrated almost exclusively on the childhood phase of human development. Various phases in the growth of children and adolescents were studied in great detail. When crises or neurotic disorders appeared in the life of an adult, the childhood would be explored in search of an explanation and perhaps a remedy for that person's present situation. Interest on the part of classical psychology in the span of human development ends with the transition from puberty to adolescence, that is, at the age of seventeen or eighteen.

Not until the research of C. G. Jung (1875-1961) were the horizons of psychology extended. Indeed, if Freud is the psychologist of the first half of life, Jung can rightly be called the psychologist of the second half. It was not his aim or purpose to trace the problems of adults back into their childhood, but to discover ways of helping them here and now.

This shift of attention, however, is much more than chronological; the issues most often dealt with exhibit a qualitative difference as

41

well. Freud looked only at the instinctual problems in his clients' neurotic conflicts, and these originated mostly in childhood. Jung, on the other hand, would claim that most of the problems brought into his consultation room by persons over thirty-five years of age were of a religious nature.

1. The Process of Individuation

If we wish to understand C. G. Jung's observations about the problems of midlife, we must consider at least briefly his concept of human development, which is called the process of individuation.

> I use the term "individuation" to denote the process by which a person becomes a psychological "individual", that is, a separate, indivisible unity or "whole".[1]

This process has two principal phases: expansion in the first half of life, and introversion in the second half.

In the first half of life the child begins to develop a conscious *ego* from the background of the unconscious, to which the child's life as an infant was entirely confined and from which the child now escapes. Jung describes the ego as the conscious core of the person, the gravitational center of one's actions and judgments. And so, during the child's growing years, the person is supposed to consolidate one's ego, gain a foothold in the world, and generally be able to be assertive.

In addition, the person develops a *persona,* an outward face or demeanor which is at once elastic and suited to the expectations of the outside world; it's a kind of mask by which the person can shield one's private moods and feelings from public scrutiny.[2] The persona is modeled upon the overall design or cast of the ego but adapts it to the social environment.

As a result of concentrating so much on the ego in the first half of life and creating a stable persona, those human qualities which were not adopted, turned out to be, in effect, neglected orphans. This would explain how, in every person, there emerges also the *shadow* – a mirror-image of the ego – "compounded partly of repressed, partly of unlived psychic features which, for moral, social, educational, or other reasons, were from the outset excluded from consciousness and from active participation in life and were therefore repressed or split off."[3]

The shadow usually consists not only of dark, negative qualities, but also of positive ones. Human nature is polar: every pole is in basic opposition to a counterpole. When one pole is raised into consciousness, the other is left behind in the unconscious; the more one feature of the personality is emphasized, the more intensely does the opposite feature in the unconscious take effect. This is true of the virtues [or attitude types], as well as of the four functions of consciousness, which Jung has identified as *thinking, feeling, intuition, sensation*. When, for example, a person develops intellectual faculties too one-sidedly, the person may be deluged at the unconscious level by infantile-instinctive expressions of feeling (e.g., sentimentality). However, for the most part, the qualities and behavior patterns making up the shadow are projected onto other persons, especially those of an opposite type. Such projection, which inhibits the shadow's entry into conscious awareness, is frequently a cause of interpersonal tensions.

Besides our own personal shadow, we also carry around a collective shadow, which is made up of the general evil – the dark side – of human history. This collective shadow is part of the collective unconscious, a repository of the experiences of the whole human race, which in turn can be variously expressed in the myths, archetypes, and symbols of religion. To the collective unconscious belong also the *anima* and the *animus*. These are defined as the archetypal composites of those special qualities which we consider feminine and masculine, motherly and fatherly.

The typical person during the first half of life is so busily occupied with self-assertion that the person identifies mostly with one's conscious ego. While repressing the shadow, the anima (or animus), and even the unconscious generally, the person suffers no great harm. All this must change in the second half of life. There's a manifold task to be done: integrating one's shadow and one's anima (or animus, in the case of a woman) into one's self-image. This means that we must draw back out outward projections, open up to our own unconscious, and make ourselves aware of the attitudes and qualities which lie therein. The ego must revert to its origin, to the *self*, in order to be revitalized. For, indeed, the main goal of individuation is a well-rounded, well-integrated self. Jung has defined the self "as the psychic totality of the individual."[4] Thus, while the ego belongs to the conscious mind and the shadow to the unconscious, the self is comprised of both.

There exists the potential, then, to expand from the ego to the self – a goal made increasingly attainable by a deeper awareness of the unconscious and a personal desire for integration.

2. The Problems of Midlife

The midlife period, roughly between the ages of thirty-five and forty-five, is that turning point at which the work of developing the ego must give way to the work of maturing the self. Yet the basic problem at this juncture is that the person believes it's possible, with the means and principles of the first half of life, to master the tasks of the second. Human life can be likened to the course of the sun. In early morning it rises and illumines the world. At midday it reaches its apex, but already the next moment it begins to pull back its rays and go down. The afternoon is just as important as the forenoon. The only difference is that it follows different laws. The respect for our own life curve means that, after midlife, we ought to adapt ourselves less to the outer and more to the inner reality. "What youth found and must find outside, the person of life's afternoon must find within."[5] So, instead of expanding, reduction to the essentials is now one's portion in life: the inward path, or, as Jung himself calls it, introversion.

The problems confronting a person at the noonday of life are related to the tasks which await the person in the second half and to which the person must adapt anew:

a) relativization of the persona,
b) acceptance of the shadow,
c) integration of anima and animus, and
d) completion of the self by acceptance of death and the encounter with God.

a) Relativization of the persona

It has cost energy, as a youth and young adult, to secure one's position in life. The struggle to assert one's claims and get ahead in the world required a stable persona. However, the business of establishing the persona took little account of how the unconscious was being repressed. If the unconscious now erupts in midlife, it throws the person off balance. The person's mental attitude collapses, the person feels disoriented and insecure. Such a loss of equilibrium is no small event; and yet, as Jung points out, it does serve a purpose. The appropriate response is to seek a new equilibrium in which the unconscious now also may hold its rightful place.[6]

True, the breakdown of the conscious attitude can also lead to catastrophe. A frequent reaction, under the guise of protecting oneself from a maelstrom of uncertainty, is to cling tenaciously to one's persona, to the identity one has acquired by reason of office, occupation, or title. Jung suggests that this identification with social or occupational status has something seductive about it,

> which is precisely why so many men are nothing more than the decorum accorded them by society. In vain would one look for a personality behind this husk. Underneath all the padding one would find a very pitiable little creature. That is why the office – or whatever this outer husk may be – is so attractive: it offers easy compensation for personal deficiencies." [7]

Instead of paying so much attention to what the world demands and taking shelter behind their personas, men and women of middle age should listen more to the promptings of the inner voice and get on with the job of enriching their personalities from deeper levels not so easily seen.

b) *Acceptance of the shadow (the problem of opposites)*

Jung sees all of human life in terms of opposites. The unconscious stands in opposition to the conscious, the shadow to the light, the anima to the animus. Oppositeness is essential to the human condition. We only become complete, only blossom out to our full selves, when, far from rejecting these opposites, we learn to include them.

The first half of life was strongly biased in favor of the conscious mind because this was needed for the ego to be formed. The reason or intellect created certain ideals for itself, which it then pursued. All these ideals, however, are reciprocated by opposite attitudes in the unconscious. The more we try to shut them out, the more they recur in our dreams. Likewise, for every behavior pattern which we consciously lived, there resides, in the unconscious, a tendency to the contrary. Midlife requires that attention be given now to the opposite poles, that the unlived shadow be both accepted and explored.

Here we witness two very common yet defective ways of behaving in midlife.

One consists in never looking at the opposite of the ego-conscious attitude. We hold tight to old values, to principles as if under siege, to acting out the role of *laudator temporis acti*. We stiffen up, become hard and bigoted. Conduct according to the rules becomes a substitute for spiritual change.[8] Fundamentally, it's our fear-of-the-opposites problem that has left us petrified. We dread our sinister brother and refuse to acknowledge him. Of such people, Jung remarks: "There must be only one truth and one guiding principle of action, and that must be absolute; otherwise it affords no protection against the impending disaster, which is sensed everywhere save in themselves."[9]

The other way of reacting wrongly to the problem of opposites is to jettison everything that had seemed good and deserving of effort before. There comes a time for us to discover the falsity of our earlier convictions, the untruth hiding in the truth, the hatred in what we formerly thought was love. But we are mistaken if we would then lay aside all our previous ideals and try to live henceforth in total opposition to our former ego. "Changes of profession, divorces, religious convulsions, apostasies of every description, are the symptoms of this swing over to the opposite."[10] We assume that, now at last, we can live according to the values that we had hitherto repressed. But instead of integrating them, we lapse into an unlived existence and begins to repress the life which we did live. Repression is still going on; only its object has changed, producing yet another imbalance as bad as before.

Certainly the error to avoid here is to suppose that, once the opposite value is seen, the former value is abolished. The victim doesn't yet understand that no value and no truth of our life is simply negated by its opposite; but

49

rather, and more to the point, we can think of them as mutually interrelated. "Everything human is relative, because everything rests on an inner polarity."[11] The tendency to reject earlier values in favor of their opposites is, consequently, just as exaggerated as the one-sidedness that reigned when, because of pure ideals, no attention was paid to any unconscious fantasies which might call them into question. What faces us in the second half of life is not a "conversion to the opposite, but conservation of previous values together with a recognition of their opposite."[12]

c) Integration of anima and animus

One sign of the problem of opposites is that men and women at the midpoint of life suddenly take on certain characteristics of the opposite sex. Jung is very explicit: "Especially among southern races, one can observe that older women develop deep, rough voices, incipient moustaches, rather hard features and other masculine traits. On the other hand the masculine physique is toned down by feminine features, such as adiposity [fattiness] and softer facial expressions."[13] Thus to Jung it would appear that masculinity and femininity represent a definite store of substances. In the first half of life a man consumes the greater part of his masculine substance, so that, during the remainder of his life, about all he has left is the feminine substance – [while, conversely, the mature woman finds that her masculine potential is becoming more active.][14]

This change would be noticeable also in the psychic transformation which men and women in their middle years must undergo: "How often it happens that a man of forty-five or fifty winds up his business and the wife then dons the trousers and opens up a little shop where he perhaps performs the duties of a handyman. There are many women who awaken to social responsibility and social consciousness only after their fortieth year. In modern business life, especially in America, nervous breakdowns in the forties are a very common occurrence. If one examines the victims one finds that what has broken down is the masculine style of life which held the field up to now, and that what is left over is an effeminate man. Contrariwise, one can observe women in these self-same business spheres who have developed in the second half of life an uncommonly masculine tough-mindedness which thrusts the feelings and the heart aside. Very often these changes are accompanied by all sorts of catastrophes in marriage, for it is not hard to imagine what will happen when the husband discovers his tender feelings and the wife her sharpness of mind."[15]

The distinctive traits and principles which we ordinarily associate with feminine and masculine are brought together, in Jung's terminology, by the two Latin expressions *anima* and *animus*. Everyone is born with elements of both. During the first half of life, only one side is emphasized, while the other is repressed [or remains latent] in the unconscious. If the man develops only his masculinity, the anima goes back into the unconscious and then makes herself felt in moodiness and vehement emotional states (affects). "She intensifies, exaggerates, falsifies, and mythologizes all emotional relations with his work and with other people of both sexes."[16]

In the case of women, when the masculine animus is repressed, the typical result is fixed opinions. Based, as they are, on unconscious prior assumptions, these opinions refuse to be shaken. They come across as unassailable principles, never to be doubted or further analyzed: opinions held valid for their own sake.

"In intellectual women the animus encourages a critical disputatiousness and would-be highbrowism, which, however, consists essentially in harping on some irrelevant weak point and nonsensically making it the main one. Or a perfectly lucid discussion gets tangled up in the most maddening way through the introduction of a quite different and if possible perverse point of view. Without even knowing it, such women are solely intent upon exasperating the man and are, in consequence, the more completely at the mercy of the animus."[17]

If a man fails to admit his feminine side – the feelings, the creative bent, the soft spot he has in his heart – he will project these anima qualities onto women, who then begin to fascinate him. Projection invariably leads to fascination. Being in love, for example, which stirs up in young people so many strong emotions, is always bound up with projection. But in the second half of life, it's time for a man to call back this projection. He should admit to himself that everything which so attracts him to the woman is, in reality, a part of his own interior makeup. For a man concerned about his masculinity, this admission is not at all easy. Jung believes that great strength and unrelenting personal honesty are required: "To recognize the shadow I call journeyman's work; to come to terms with the anima is the work of the master, which, unfortunately, only a few ever manage to accomplish."[18]

Jung points out various ways of confronting the anima. The first step is to stop repressing my moods, my affects and emotions, either by covering them up with an occupation or by demeaning their significance – in the sense of excusing them as "just one of those weaknesses I haven't overcome." I ought, at long last, to see through this hoary old mechanism of "depreciation and denial"[19] and begin to take seriously, as objective occurrences, the manifestations of the unconscious in my moods and affects.

I ought to initiate a conversation with these moods of mine. By doing so, I give the unconscious a chance to express itself and thus to attain consciousness. By asking my clamoring emotions what they are trying to tell me, to which qualities, desires, and dispositions in my unconscious they want to call attention, I allow the anima living within me to have her say. Such a conversation with one's moods and feelings – and, in them, with one's own unconscious – is regarded by Jung as an important technique for training the anima.[20] Some other ways include the conscious exercise of one's emotional powers and the cultivation of those musical and artistic gifts that are latent in every human being.

The unconscious material which a man will confront in his anima is not without its dangers. Not only can it disturb him (who is so knowledgeable and well – adjusted in the conscious world), but it might also take over and devour. So he needs a safeguard: something to help him relate to his unconscious in a way that will produce from it some benefit.

Now, as Jung himself makes clear, this needed safeguard is provided by religion, with all its powerful symbols. Religion takes up the instinctive, intuitive, and creative themes of the anima and acts toward the man as a life-giving mother, or as a copious spring from which he may drink the essence of vitality and invention.

Religion offers him the security he looks for in the mother-figure while, at the same time, it severs the infantile bond to the natural mother from whom he was born. Anyone who remains attached to his mother is wholly at the mercy of his emotions and, says Jung, is endangering his psychic health. The mother-bond is often unconscious and asserts itself in the projection of the man's anima to a particular woman who, for him, takes on the role of mother. In midlife, as the unconscious forces itself upon him with all its unpredictability, the man reaches out for protection and safety. Fear of the unknown (the unconscious) causes him to resort to the woman's protection, and this confers on her an unwarranted, ill-fated power over him, as she gives in to her seductive and possessive instincts. Religion, Jung believes, is an effective countermeasure, allowing the man to experience the anima within him, while at the same time warding off the fascination which would otherwise occur if he projects his anima onto any specific women.

As stated before, religion opens up a way to experience all the prolific and creative forces of the anima which are essential to a man's well-being. Without the anima, he gradually suffers the loss of vitality, flexibility, and even human kindness. "The result, as a rule, is premature rigidity, crustiness, stereotypy, fanatical one-sidedness, obstinacy, and pedantry, or else resignation, weariness, sloppiness, irresponsibility, and finally a childish *ramollissement* [brain dysfunction] with a tendency to alcohol."[21]

Like the man with his anima, so must the woman learn to deal with her animus, putting it to use as an entry gate to her own unconscious, as a means of getting to know better what it contains. And her opinions, which so often have the character of solid, unshakeable convictions and eternally valid principles, never to be encroached upon, ought to be critically questioned and explored as to their origin, because, in so doing, she may discover the unconscious presuppositions lying beneath those opinions of hers which earlier seemed so rationally founded. The animus thus becomes a bridge to the unconscious, wherein the fruit-bearing and creative forces which the woman needs for self-realization are waiting to be found.

For women, religion has a somewhat different function in bringing about integration than it does for men. Of more importance for women are the ascetical and moral claims of religion; these can lead the woman out of a sheltering, too protective "motherly mode" into engagement, responsibility, and action. To the anima, the animus will provide shape and form, while the challenging Spirit descending from the Father will help the anima bear fruit. Thus can religion impart to the anima a suitable frame of reference in which to develop and grow.

A further support in the process of integrating the anima and animus is the community, which offers us not only the elements of challenge and form, but security as well. Should we pull away from the community, we cut ourselves off from the mainstream of life. Jung would attribute this kind of self-isolation to the concealing of affects, as, for example, a feeling of inferiority. Thus the root cause of isolation and loneliness is not really a lack of sociability, but of humility. Anyone too proud to open up to other human beings is indeed self-isolating, but the person who is open and humble enough never feels alone.[22]

In summary, then, whoever allows their persona, constructed for its outward appearance, to be broken through again and again by the confrontational forces of the anima and animus, whoever faces up honestly to their own polarities, whoever continues to inquire into their feelings and opinions, whoever is humble and unassuming enough to open oneself up to others – such a one the community can effectively support in the labor of integrating anima and animus and of placing them in spiritual equilibrium.

d) Completion of the self by acceptance of death and the encounter with God

The real problem facing us in midlife is our basic attitude toward death. The psychophysical curve of life, now bending downward, hastens toward its end. Only for the believer in life after death is the terminus of this present life a sensible goal. Only for the believer does the second half of life have inherent meaning and purpose. Existence after death is not so much a matter of religious faith, says Jung, but of psychic reality. The soul finds it reasonable. And so, while preparing itself for death, the soul remains healthy.[23]

Midlife is the time when we must come to friendly terms with death. We must consciously accept the decline of our biological life curve, for then only can our psychological line reach higher in the direction of individuation. Jung observes: "From the middle of life onward, only this person remains vitally alive who is ready to die with life."[24] In his work *The Soul and Death [Seele und Tod]*, Jung goes on to describe the fear of dying as a correlate of the fear of living:

> Many young people have at bottom a panic fear of life (though at the same time they intensely desire it), and an even greater number of the aging have the same fear of death. Indeed, I have known those people who most feared life when they were young to suffer later just as much from fear of death. When they are young one says they have infantile resistance against the normal demands of life; one should really say the same thing when they are old, for they are likewise afraid of one of life's normal demands. We are so convinced that death is simply the end of a process that it does not ordinarily occur to us to conceive of death as a goal and a fulfillment, as we do without hesitation the aims and purposes of youthful life in its ascendance.[25]

Life is directed toward a goal. In youth the goal is to become established in the world and to achieve something. With midlife, the goal changes. It's no longer at the summit but in the valley: there where the ascent began.

So, the question is: are we making progress toward this goal? When we do not move on, clinging feverishly to our [past or present] life, we will experience a discrepancy between our psychological life curve and our biological. "Consciousness stays up in the air, while the curve of the parabola sinks downward with ever-increasing speed."[26] In the last analysis, a person's refusing to die is *not wanting to live.* Only by accepting the law of life, by moving toward death as an appropriate goal, can we remain truly alive and grow to a ripe maturity.

Instead of looking ahead to the goal of death, many fix their eyes on what is finished and past. While we all pity the infantile person of thirty who looks back nostalgically to childhood, society today bestows wonder and praise on septuagenarians who appear to be young people and who act just as they did years ago.

Yet, remarks Jung, "both are perverse, lacking in style, psychological monstrosities. A young person who does not fight and conquer has missed the best part of youth, and an older person who does not know how to listen to the secrets of the brooks, as they tumble . . . from the peaks to the valleys, makes no sense; the person is a spiritual mummy who is nothing but . . . a relic of the past. The person stands apart from life, mechanically repeating oneself to the last triviality."[27] What kind of culture is it that needs shadowy characters like this?

Grasping for the days of youth while one is advancing in years is an everyday sign of dreading the future. Jung asks rhetorically: "Who does not know those touching old gentlemen who must always warm up the dish of their student days, who can fan the flame of life only by reminiscences of their heroic youth, but who, for the rest, are stuck in a hopeless wooden Philistinism?"[28] Instead of preparing for old age, they become perpetual youngsters – in Jung's opinion, a "lamentable substitute for the illumination of the self,"[29] which is required of men and women in the second half of life.

People in midlife today are not prepared for what awaits them. As a reason, Jung claims that we indeed have schools for young people, but not for the forty-year-olds, to teach them something about the second half of life. From ages past, the religions were such schools, giving instruction and sharing insights as to the mysteries of growing old. And even today, Jung can recommend to the person in midlife no other school than those religions which teach the art of dying, which hold out a program leading beyond self-assertiveness in the world to a new realm where the individual for the first time can fully and truly become a human being.

According to Jung, there can be no expansion of the self until one has acquired an intimate sense of the divine indwelling. The idea of "God within us" as taught by St. Paul ("No longer do I live, but Christ lives in me") expresses for Jung the experience of a man or a women who has sorted himself or herself out.

The challenge for us in midlife is to let go of our narrow ego and submit ourselves to God. But if we should refuse, how shall we ever find our way to wholeness or, for lacking that, our way to spiritual health? The problem facing so many people is actually a religious one, as Jung the physician points out:

> Among all my patients in the second half of life – that is to say, over thirty-five – there has not been one whose problem in the last resort was not that of finding a religious outlook . . . . It is safe to say that every one of them fell ill because they had lost what the living religions of every age have given to their followers, and none of them has been really healed who did not regain their religious outlook.[30]

For one's encounter with the divine archetype, an experience leading to psychological health, Jung recommends many of the same techniques as we find among the spiritual writers. Citing an elaborate fantasy about a sacrifice, he interprets the hero or heroine as giving himself or herself over to God, offering up some of his or her ego, and then gaining himself or herself in return. The practice of introversion, which Jung considers a normal demand of midlife, is done best in meditation and asceticism:

> Solitude and fasting have from time immemorial been the best known means of strengthening any meditation whose purpose is to open the door to the unconscious.[31]

This descent to the unconscious – a search of one's inner depths – produces renewal and spiritual rebirth. The treasure spoken of by Christ lies hidden in the unconscious; only by the symbols and rites of religion can we lift this treasure up. Just as Christ, through death, descended into the netherworld, so too must we all make our journey through the night of the unconscious, through the frightening ordeal of self-encounter, in order that, strengthened by the powers of the unconscious, we might all be born again.[32]

Those who have endured the crises of midlife can speak of the changes which, to some degree at least, they permitted God to work in them – if through nothing more than the symbolism of dreams and visions. Some of the transformations recounted to Jung by his clients are captured by Jung in this summary:

> They came to themselves, they could accept themselves, they were able to become reconciled to themselves, and thus they were also reconciled to adverse circumstances and events. This is quite similar to what was formerly expressed by saying: We have made our peace with God, we have sacrificed our own will, we have submitted ourselves to the will of God.[33]

Spiritual rebirth – openness to God's transforming grace – is the challenge of the second half of life. Accompanied no doubt by danger, it is also filled with promise. Very little psychological knowledge as such is required; far more important is true piety – a readiness to turn inward and listen attentively to the God who dwells within us. This, after all, is what religious devotion should really mean. With great spiritual effort, says Jung, the person who arrives at the noonday of life should be dedicated from that time onward to the task of complete self-realization. It's a challenging task which we obviously cannot manage by our own strength but at which – God willing – we can succeed.

Bibliographical Notes

The translators have checked for American or British editions of the works cited by Grün to the extent it was practical to do so and then, for the passages quoted from these works, have used any existing translations that seemed both clear and accurate. Footnotes have been adapted accordingly and the bibliography has been enlarged for the reader's convenience.

The source most often cited for John Tauler's sermons is the collection compiled and translated by I. Weilner in *Johannes Taulers Bekehrungsweg: Die Erfahrungsgrundlagen seiner Mystik* (Regensburg, 1961). Since this work is not available in English, the author's own method of citing it is retained: page numbers corresponding to Weilner's numbering are shown in parentheses at the end of a cited passage. Other sources and allusions (with a few not acknowledged by the author) are referenced in the footnotes.

ABBREVIATIONS

JTP Tauler, Johannes. *PREDIGTEN*. Vollständige Ausgabe, übertragen u. hrsg. von G. Hofmann. Freiburg: Herder, 1961.

CWE Jung, C. G. *THE COLLECTED WORKS OF C. G. JUNG*. Translated by R. F. C. Hull. (Bollingen Series XX). 2nd ed. Princeton, NJ: Princeton University Press, 1966-1979.

Vol. 5 **Symbols of Transformation**
(New York: Pantheon, 1956; 2nd ed., 1967)

Vol. 7 **Two Essays on Analytical Psychology**
(1953; 2nd ed., 1966)

Vol. 8 **The Structure and Dynamics of the Psyche** (1960; 2nd ed., 1969)

Vol. 9 Part 1. **The Archetypes and the Collective Unconscious** (1959; 2nd ed., 1968)

Vol. 9 Part 2. **Aion: Researches into the Phenomenology of the Self** (1959; 2nd ed., 1968)

Vol. 11 **Psychology and Religion: West and East** (New York: Pantheon, 1958; 2nd ed., 1969)

GWG Jung, C. G. *GESAMMELTE WERKE.* **5.** Bd., **7.** Bd., n.p.; **8.** Bd., Zürich & Stuttgart: Rascher Verlag, 1967; Olten: Walter Verlag, 1971; **9.** Bd., Olten & Freiburg im Br.: Walter, 1976; **11.** Bd., Zürich & Stuttgart: Rascher, 1963; Olten & Freiburg im Br.: Walter, 1971.

INTRODUCTION and
I. SURVIVING THE ORDEAL OF MIDLIFE
(Tauler)

1 "The Stages of Life," *CWE* 8, pp. 387-403, #749-795. [Hull's translation of this essay is based on that of W. S. Dell and Cary F. Baynes in *Modern Man in Search of a Soul* (London: Routledge, 1933-1959). "Die Lebenswende", *GWG* 8, ss. 441-460. Additional titles on the same subject, in German and English, are detailed in the Supplementary Bibliography.]

2 *JTP*, ss. 136f. (Sermon 19). [English translations of this sermon are found in Shrady (pp. 72-73) and in Strokosch (p. 61). The Shrady book contains also the sermons quoted hereinafter on pp. 16-17 (Weilner, 177; Shrady, 151), on pp. 21-22 (Weilner, 154; Shrady, 63-64), and on p. 38, (*JTP*, 19; Shrady, 40). See the Supplementary Bibliography.]

3 Weilner, s. 174. In presenting Tauler's thought we depend mostly on the work of Weilner, who has ex-

plained very well how the sermons of Tauler develop in a spiritual sense the meaning of the various stages of life.

4   [Our translation of the extended passage about self-made cisterns (from Sermon 18) is revised from that of Maria Shrady, *Sermons of Johannes Tauler* (New York: Paulist Press, 1985), pp. 63-64. – Trans.]

5   *JTP*, s. 523 (Sermon 68).

6   *JTP*, ss. 625f. (Sermon 84).

7   *JTP*, s. 339 (Sermon 44).

8   *JTP*, s. 626 (Sermon 84). Tauler quotes somewhat freely the passage in Book 2 of the *Dialogues* where Pope St. Gregory the Great tells how Benedict, after overcoming temptation, became a teacher of the spiritual life. The passage reads in English: "Now that he was free from these temptations, he was ready to instruct others in the practice of virtue. That is why Moses commanded the Levites to begin their service no sooner than the age of twenty-five, and to become guardians of the sacred vessels only after the age of fifty" (cf. Numbers 8:24-26). [See also the translation by Odo J. Zimmerman *et al.* (New York: Fathers of the Church, Inc., 1959), p. 60. The versions by Gardner (1911) and Uhlfelder (1967) are less satisfactory.]

9   *JTP*, s. 626 (Sermon 84).

10 Carlo Carretto, *Wo der Dornbusch brennt,* (Freiburg: Herder, 1976), ss. 81f.

11 *JTP*, s. 19 (Sermon 1).   12 Ibid., s. 18.

II. PROBLEMS OF MIDLIFE (Jung)

1   *GWE* 9:1, p. 275, #490; *GWG* 9:1, s. 293.

2   Jolande [S.] Jacobi, *The Way of Individuation,* trans. by R. F. C. Hull (Harcourt, Brace & World,

c.1967; reprinted New York: New American Library, 1983), p. 37. *Der Weg zur Individuation* (Zürich: Rascher, 1965), s. 48f. On the practical necessity of a well-fitting persona, see *CWE* 7, pp. 192ff., #305ff.; *GWG* 7, s. 218. [Grün depends very much in this section on Jacobi's coherent, authoritative presentation of Jung's ideas. Her chapters devoted to the main phases of the individuation process, their stages, and the notions of ego and self, pp. 21-59, are especially recommended. – Translators]

3 Jacobi, *Way*, p. 38; Jacobi, *Weg*, s. 50.

4 *CWE* 11 (1st ed., Pantheon Books, 1958), p. 156, #232; *GWG* 11, s. 170.

5 *CWE* 7, p. 75, #114; *GWG* 7, s. 81.

6 *CWE* 7, pp. 163f., #254; *GWG* 7, ss. 178f.

7 *CWE* 7, p. 145, #230; *GWG* 7, s. 159.

8 *CWE* 9:1, p. 136, #243; *GWG* 9:1, s. 151.

9 *CWE* 7, p. 76, #116; *GWG* 7, s. 82.

10 *CWE* 7, p. 75, #115; *GWG* 7, s. 81. [The entire discussion of the second reaction to opposites, when not quoted verbatim, is paraphrased by the author from paragraph #115 in Jung. – Translators]

11 *CWE* 7, p. 75, #115; *GWG* 7, s. 82.

12 *CWE* 7, p. 76, #116; *GWG* 7, s. 82.

13 *CWE* 8, pp. 397-398, #780; *GWG* 8, ss. 453f.

14 *CWE* 8, p. 398, #782; *GWG* 8, s. 454.

15 *CWE* 8, p. 398, #783; *GWG* 8, ss. 454f.

16 *CWE* 9:1, p. 70, #144; *GWG* 9:1, s. 86.

17 *CWE* 7, p. 208, #335; *GWG* 7, s. 229. [The foregoing description of fixed opinions is adapted from pp. 206ff., #331ff.]

18 C. G. Jung, *Briefe* (III, 1956-1961), trans. & ed. Aniela Jaffé and Gerhard Adler (Olten & Freiburg

im Br.: Walter Verlag, c.1973, 3rd ed. 1980-81), s. 225. C. G. Jung, *Letters*, ed. Gerhard Adler with Aniela Jaffé, translations from German by R. F. C. Hull (2 vols., Bollingen Series XCV; Princeton, NJ: Princeton University Press, 1973, 1984, 1986). [This letter was not found in English; only Vol. 1 (1906-50) was available to the translators.]

19 *CWE* 7, p. 202, #323; *GWG* 7, s. 222.

20 *CWE* 7, pp. 203, 215-216, #323, 345-350; *GWG* 7, ss. 223, 237.

21 *CWE* 9:1, p. 71, #147; *GWG* 9:1, s. 87.

22 C. G. Jung, *Briefe* (III, 1956-1961), s. 93. [This letter was not found in English. Only Volume 1 of the *Letters* (1906-1950) was available. Jung's advice: "When you are lonely, the reason is that you isolate yourself. If you are humble and ordinary enough, you will never suffer loneliness. Nothing isolates us more than power and prestige. So try to climb down, learn humility, and you'll never be alone." – Translators]

23 "The Soul and Death," *CWE* 8, pp. 404ff., #796ff., pp. 408-409, #803ff.; *GWG* 8, ss. 457ff., 469ff.

24 Ibid., p. 407, #800; ibid., s. 466.

25 Ibid., p. 405, #797; ibid., s. 465.

26 Ibid., p. 406, #799; ibid., s. 464.

27 Ibid., p. 407, #801; ibid., s. 466.

28 Ibid., p. 396, #776; ibid., s. 452.

29 Ibid., p. 399, #785; ibid., s. 455. [The following paragraph, concerning schools for 40-year-olds, is adapted from pp. 398-399, #784, 786.]

30 *CWE* 11 (1st ed., Pantheon Books, 1958), p. 334, #509; *GWG* (Zürich & Stuttgart, 1963), s. 362.

31 *CWE* 5 (1st ed., Pantheon Books, 1956), p. 335, #518; *GWG* 5, s. 428. [In the immediate context

of this advice, Jung is commenting on the epic hero of Longfellow's *The Song of Hiawatha,* who "builds himself a hut in the forest in order to fast and have dreams and visions." *CWE* 5, p. 334, #517.]

[32] [This paragraph is a Christian application of Jung's treatise on Hiawatha and his experience of regression. Cf. *CWE* 5, pp. 330-339, #508-526.]

[33] C. G. Jung, *Psychology and Religion* (New Haven: Yale University Press, c.1938, 1969), p. 99. Jung, *Psychologie und Religion* (Zürich, 1947), s. 147. [For a later revision of the Yale text, see *CWE* 11, pp. 81-82, #138. Our version is a composite. – Trans.]

SUPPLEMENTARY BIBLIOGRAPHY

Bianchi, Eugene C. *On Growing Older: A Personal Guide to Life After Thirty-Five.* New York, NY: Crossroad, 1986.

Bovet, Theodor. *Führung durch die Lebensalter: Weg und Sinn.* 2. Auflage, Bern: Haupt, c.1955, 1964; 3. Aufl., Tübingen: Katzmann, 1967.

Carretto, Carlo. *The God Who Comes.* Translated by Rose Mary Hancock from *Il Dio Che Viene.* Maryknoll, NY: Orbis Books, c.1974.

_____. *The Desert in the City.* Translated by Barbara Wall from *Il Deserto Nella Citta.* New York: Wm. Collins Publishers, 1979.

_____. *In Search of the Beyond.* Translated by Sarah Fawcett from *Al de la delle Cose.* Maryknoll, NY: Orbis Books, 1976.

David, J. "Altersrevolution: statt Abbau Veränderung," in *Orientierung* 38 (1974): 151-154.

Guardini, Romano. *Die Lebensalter: Ihre ethische und pädagogische Bedeutung.* 4. Aufl., Würzburg: Werkbund Verlag, 1957; 7. Aufl., 1963.

_____. *Les âges de la vie.* Translated by G. Bousquet. Paris: Éditions du Cerf, 1956; re-edition, 1965.

Heydt, Vera von der. *Prospects for the Soul: Soundings in Jungian Psychology and Religion.* London: Darton, Longman and Todd, 1976.

Hulme, William E. *Mid-Life Crises.* Philadelphia: The Westminster Press, c.1980.

O'Collins, Gerald. *The Second Journey.* New York: The Paulist Press, c.1978.

Pöggeler, Franz. *Die Lebensalter.* Mainz: n. p., 1973.

Schreiber, Hermann. *Midlife Crisis: Die Krise in der Mitte des Lebens.* München: Bertelsmann, 1977.

_____. *La crisis de la mediana edad.* Translated by Alfredo N. Báez. Buenos Aires: Crea, 1978.

Sheehy, Gail. *Pathfinders.* New York: Morrow, 1981.

Stein, Murray. *In Midlife: A Jungian Perspective.* Dallas: Spring Publications, c.1983.

Tauler, Johann. *Sermons.* Translated and edited by Maria Shrady. (Classics of Western Spirituality, No. 48). New York: Paulist Press, 1985.

_____. *Signposts to Perfection: A Selection from the Sermons of Johann Tauler.* Translated and edited by Elizabeth Strakosch. St. Louis: B. Herder, 1958.

Tauler, John [O.P.]. *Spiritual Conferences.* Translated and edited by Eric Colledge & Sr. M. Jane, O.P. (Cross & Crown Series, No. 20). St. Louis: B. Herder, c.1961. [Sermons compiled from *Die Predigten Taulers*. Vol. 11: *Deutsche Texte des Mittelalters,* publ. Ferdinand Vetter, 1910.]

Tournier, Paul. *The Adventure of Living*. Translated by Edwin Hudson from *L'Aventure de la vie*. New York: Harper & Row, 1965.

_____. *The Healing of Persons*. Translated by Edwin Hudson. New York: Harper & Row, c.1965, 1963.

_____. *The Person Reborn*. Translated by Edwin Hudson. London: SCM Press & Heinemann, 1967.

_____. *The Seasons of Life*. Translated by John S. Gilmour from *Les saisons de la vie* (Geneva: Éditions Labor et Fides, 1961). Richmond, VA: John Knox Press, 1963; 5th printing, 1967. New York: Pillar Books, 1976.

_____. *Die Jahreszeiten unseres Lebens: Entfaltung und Erfüllung*. Hamburg: Furche Verlag, 1967. [But published originally as *Lebensentfaltung und Lebenserfüllung: vom Sinn unseres Lebens*. Hamburg: Furche Verlag, 1960.]

Van Kaam, Adrian, C.S.Sp. *The Transcendent Self: Formative Spirituality of the Middle, Early, and Later Years of Life*. Denville, NJ: Dimension Books, c.1979.

Vollmer, H. *Die Krise in den mittleren Jahren und wie sie zu bewältigen ist*. München: n. p., 1977.

Wulf, F. "Der Mittagsdämon oder die Krise der Lebensmitte," in *Geist und Leben* 38 (1965): 241-245.

SCHUYLER SPIRITUAL SERIES

Vol. 01 Grün/Scharper, **Benedict of Norcia**   Order-No. 10-001
(with The Legacy of Benedict)   PB (1992) 108 p. **$ 3.95**

Vol. 02 Ruppert/Grün, **Christ in the Brother**   Order-No. 10-002
(According to the Rule of St. Benedict)   PB (1992) 61 p. **$ 3.60**

Vol. 03 Clifford Stevens, **Intimacy with God**   Order-No. 10-003
(Notes on the Vocation to Celibacy)   PB (1992) 120 p. **$ 3.95**

Vol. 04 Clifford Stevens, **The Noblest Love**   Order-No. 10-004
(The Sacramentality of Sex in Marriage)   PB (1992) 82 p. **$ 3.70**

Vol. 05 Grün, **Dreams on the Spiritual Journey** Order-No. 10-005
     PB (1993) 72 p. **$ 4.00**

Vol. 06 Grün, **The Eucharist and Spiritual Growth** Order-No. 10-006
     PB (1993) 96 p. **$ 5.00**

Vol. 07 Grün, **Prayer and Self-knowledge**   Order-No. 10-007
     PB (1993) 72 p. **$ 4.50**

Vol. 08 Grün, **Celibacy - a fullness of life**   Order-No. 10-008
     PB (1993) 96 p. **$ 5.00**

Vol. 09 Colombás, **Reading God**   Order-No. 10-009
(Lectio divina)   PB (1993) 144 p. **$ 5.50**

Vol. 10 Grün, **The Challenge of Midlife**   Order-No. 10-010
     PB (1993) 72 p. **$ 4.50**

Vol. 11 Grün, **The Challenge of Silence**   Order-No. 10-011
     PB (1993) 72 p. **$ 4.50**

Vol. 12 Grün/Dufner, **Health as a Spiritual Task** Order-No. 10-012
     PB (1993) 96 p. **$ 5.00**

Additional Books from BMH-Publications:

Sr. Mary James Uhing, **Windows of a Heart**   Order-No. 20-001
(A book of poetry), illustrated.   PB (1993) 72 p. **$ 5.00**

The Rosary   HC (1988) 400 p. **Order-No. 20-002**   **$ 10.00**
153 full color ilustrations of the life of Jesus and Mary.

The Holy Mass HC (1993) 448 p. **Order-No. 20-003**   **$ 12.00**
(in Word and Picture), 214 full color illustrations.